SIDEWALKS

RON GAVALIK

Pittsburgh Poet

Published by Pittsburgh Poet
Pittsburgh, Pennsylvania
Author: Ron Gavalik
Proofreading and Editing: Rebecca Hoffman
Cover and Book Layout: Pittsburgh Poet Contributors

ISBN-13: 978-1-7320697-0-1

Experience more works by Ron Gavalik at
PittsburghPoet.com

For the bad motherfuckers,
the men and women of substance
who walk upon sidewalks
in search of a better life.

One hundred years ago, my great grandfather walked on sidewalks to the street car that carried him and so many others to the coal mines. As wage servants, those men broke their bodies and lost their souls under the most hateful conditions, all for the pennies their wives used to keep them fed, functional, alive. My grandfather walked on sidewalks to the steel mill, and to the back alley dice games. My father walked on sidewalks to the rail yards and to the Slovak club for cheap beers and priceless friendships. Today, we walk on sidewalks to bus stops, restaurants, museums, and parks. The jobs are safer. We work out in gyms to become sculpted, sexier. Overall, our moods and lifespans have improved, but the subtle desperation of our forebears has remained.

The free verse poems before you in this collection are a combination of observations, personal truths, and the experiences of a writer born and raised in Pittsburgh, Pennsylvania. The creative process required two years of long whiskey nights, during the most turbulent times of my life.

The extraction of memories from one's guts to create consumable poetry is a messy business, and I never could have completed it on my own. Rebecca Hoffman is a dedicated editor. She's the only person alive I trust with my work from its metamorphosis of fragile words to the music of our human condition. The authors who've endorsed this collection pour their hearts into their written works. I consider myself fortunate to simply know these people.

It's now time to begin. You and I, we're about to stroll along strange sidewalks never before traveled to explore the horrors of our truths and the sadness of our lies. We'll laugh and cry, think and pray. In the end, we'll have become better friends, lovers, allies ready to do battle with a world fixed on hate.

—Ron Gavalik

ACT ONE

Degenerate

I'm the degenerate you love to hate,
the unclean sinner who won't toe the line.
You ridicule my independence at dinner parties,
among similarly dressed cronies,
the institutionalized prisoners
of prestige.

Hate us all, the degenerates.
Scorn the indie musician on the sidewalk.
He colors the dull march of the khakis.
Despise the painter in welfare housing.
She strokes thick lines of anguish
onto uncomfortable canvases.
Taunt the quiet poet at the end of the bar.
He writes raw truth on napkins gone ignored.

Loathe the degenerates you secretly fuck
when fashionable friends aren't looking.
Eyes fixed on your contemptuous smirk,
I am unable to cast judgment upon you.
Another degenerate spreads her tattooed thighs
without any hope of acceptance.
She only wishes to feel for a moment
the intoxicating sensation
of your temporary love.

The degenerate's climax is the richest syrup
that briefly covers your vanilla routines.
Debauchery provides you a moment
to feel freedom within slums,
the pleasures of darkness,
and the uninhibited passions of life
without approval.

Lego Man

Many years ago,
while taking an early spring walk
near the University of Pittsburgh,
I noticed a deep crack in the sidewalk,
and within the crevice
someone had wedged a Lego action figure.
I considered removing the toy
as a keepsake of the first day outside
after a brutal winter,
but instead I allowed it to remain
as a small part of the urban landscape.
For several years, I took early spring walks
along the same part of the city,
and every year the Lego man,
a little more weathered,
greeted me as an old acquaintance.
Eventually, the city replaced the sidewalk,
and like so many loose friendships,
based on convenience and circumstance,
the Lego man was gone.

Weather Observation

The raindrops that fell
against the window this morning
were in perfect sync
with the coffee drips that fell
into my cup.
Down on the sidewalk,
a man in a suit and a woman in a dress
scurried toward a church under an umbrella.
I watched for them to march in lockstep,
but it never happened.
Sometimes we thirst for the simplicity
of order,
and other times we quietly celebrate
the chaos.

Suspicion

A brown and white cat
on the sidewalk
licked its back.
I said 'hello.'
The cat stopped
and stared at me.
It didn't trust people.
Smart cat.

Make It

The faces on sidewalks
change daily,
but the people
remain the same.
Sinners, saints,
all of us
trying to make it,
and all of us
will eventually
die trying.

So Much Beauty

There is so much beauty in this world,
and it exists all around us.
The old tree along the road,
its imperfect trunk has endured many winters.
The curvaceous young woman on the sidewalk,
she swings her hips as a gift
to all who take notice.
The priest with a hand pressed against the wall,
he prays for us all.
There is so much beauty in this world,
one really must work hard
to avoid it.

Vodka Blowjobs

In the mid-1990s, I worked as a bartender
on the second floor of a local hotdog joint
near the University of Pittsburgh.
I poured beers and mixed simple drinks
for working class drunks.
The felons always had a game or a magic trick
they'd use to milk rubes for a free gin and tonic.
College students mostly stayed away,
but the ones who stumbled in only ordered drafts,
paid for by daddy's allowance
or the petty drug rackets they ran on campus.
In the summer, the best sluts came around,
tits pushed out of their tops,
ass cheeks crept below their skirts.
They knew how to find action
every single night.

Except one overweight girl named Susie
from the smaller, all girl's school down the road.
She'd come to the bar alone,
her lips caked with dark red lipstick.
Like many students, Susie wanted to be older.
She'd order vodka martinis,
drink quietly, and she'd patiently wait
for one of the older drunks to make a move.
It never happened.

Sometimes Susie complained to me
about other girls at her college,
that they were aggressive lesbians.
All of them wanted to eat her snatch.
'Those bitches are as bad as the men,' she'd say.
But then she'd laugh it off.
'I really love cock,' she told me.

'I think about cock and cum all the time.'

One night Susie owed the bar $27.50.
She always tried to flirt her way past the tab.
I never let her get away with it.
'Do you like me?' she said.
I laid down my trademark response,
'You're the best.'
'No, do you really like me?'
I figured she deserved a real compliment.
'You have the sexiest lips here.'

She climbed off the barstool
and walked to the back door, the fire escape.
She then curled her finger at me to join her.
Outside on the small rusted iron landing,
above the roach-filled dumpster,
Susie crouched between my legs.
Both of us worked to unbuckle my belt.
A swarm of hands pulled down my jeans.
I looked up at the few stars between buildings
as those red lips and soft tongue became my drug,
a back alley escape from a bullshit life.
When I unloaded, she refused to let go.
$27.50 paid in full,
plus tip.

That's how we went for a while.
I gave Susie small escapes from lesbians.
Susie gave me small escapes from life.
Eventually, she stopped coming around.
I figured she graduated.
Perhaps her classmates finally got their wish.
Either way, I never saw her again.

Splendors

Near our house when I was a child,
the roots of a massive tree had lifted
the slab of a sidewalk several inches.
The kids in the neighborhood,
we'd ride our bikes fast over the slab
and catch air as fearless daredevils
on our way to the local park and ball field.

One spring day in the city,
I tripped on a similarly lifted slab.
I almost went down like a sack of bricks,
which would have shattered my ego
along with the overpriced smartphone
in my pocket.

I cursed the city for not repairing
the obvious safety hazard.
It wasn't until I got home
that I realized I'd sold out
the small joys and the imagination
sparked by the world's imperfections
for the false splendors
of modern life.

Words of the Prophets

Sitting in the diner at 4:00 AM,
it's just me and the waitress,
and the trucker in the back booth
slowly sipping his coffee.
The waitress says she can't wait
until dawn so she can leave.
I don't have the heart to tell her
the trucker and I are desperately hanging on
to the last glimpses of moonlight.

Across the street, spray-painted words
are scrawled across a concrete wall
that read, 'Live for today
because there is no tomorrow.'
Prophetic truths
that do not lead to tangible improvements
often lose their meaning, their power.
Communities lost and without direction
begin to decay.

Old Woman

I stood on the sidewalk
in front of the cigar shop on South Side,
hands in my pockets,
my surroundings tinted blue.
After a lifetime of struggle
with depression and narcissism,
so many shit men
and far too many shit jobs,
her body finally surrendered
to time.

An old woman approached,
with long, braided gray hair
and small, round sunglasses,
the kind of hip senior citizen
I wish *she* could have been.
The old woman,
without saying a word,
patted my arm.
That stranger understood
my torment,
she knew
my pain.

Write My Music

On late Saturday nights
under the magnificent city skyline,
the young kill themselves
at varying rates of speed.
The old lie awake in their beds,
reminiscent of the better times.
All I can do is write my music
between mouthfuls of bourbon
and remember why I love you.

Living Art

There's a beauty that emerges
within those who have the courage
to break with conventional thinking.

The worker who finally tells off the boss,
no one owns him.
The slut who ignores the shaming,
she enjoys being enjoyed.
The father who embraces his gay son,
his career status be damned.

That flicker of confidence
in the eyes of those who awaken
to their truths
is living art, a gift
that each of us
can experience.

Hello, Dog

A big black dog without a leash
walked up to me on the sidewalk.
'Hello, dog,' I said.
It didn't sniff me or lick me,
but instead sat right next to me
and leaned against my leg.

My first thought was that the
spirit of my late father or grandfather
had come to check up on me,
and for a moment, the stress
of the bills and the job were gone.

Then a young guy in a designer track suit
and moussed hair jogged toward us.
The dog got excited, jumped up,
and took off down the sidewalk.
'I hope he didn't bother you,'
the guy said as he ran past.
'Nope. He made my day.'

Orange Fuck

Sipping a coffee
while sitting at a sidewalk table
in front of a coffee shop on Pittsburgh's South Side,
a flamboyant young man
spoke about local gay culture
to a young woman.

'What is wrong with people?' he said.
'If I want to suck some dick,' he shouted ,
'my mother's friends don't need to watch.
Why should they care?'
The young woman chuckled,
and then laughed out loud.
'I mean, who do you have to fuck around here
to get a little respect?'

I quickly Googled a photo of Donald Trump
on my smartphone and pointed it at the man.
'You gotta fuck this guy,' I said.
'Absolutely not,' he said.
'I better stick to the human race.'

Emasculated

A young man and woman,
their arms, necks, and cheeks
covered in tattoos,
argued hard
in front of a store's sidewalk sale.
The guy said he had enough.
He then grabbed the girl by the arm
and dragged her a couple of feet.
The girl dropped her backpack,
and then she planted a combat boot
on his leg, near his balls.

'What the fuck, Caroline?'
'I fuck who I want,' she said,
'and if you don't like it, fucking leave.'
The young guy stood there quiet,
his balls tucked neatly in the girl's bag
as she casually browsed through
a collection of purses.

Red Pumps

During the spring and early summer months one year,
a crazy old man hung around a small parking lot
on Pittsburgh's South Side.
Usually, he mumbled to himself.
Sometimes he shouted incomprehensible
insults and warnings of damnation
to random people that walked by.

The old man always wore a knit skullcap
and a Navy pea coat, as if he were shipping out to sea.
Below the waist, he strutted around in ladies capri pants
with a colorful flower print,
and his hairy feet bulged out of a pair
of red hot stripper pumps.

Apparently, that old man wanted to stay warm
while he played watchman over the city,
but nothing beat the power of sexy.

Working Man

A man goes to work.
He sells his skills, his talents,
his motherfucking soul.
He pounds sidewalks, rides on buses,
flies on planes, and he drives in endless traffic.
The working man sacrifices
day after day
for his family.

On his own, that man will game the system,
he'll do what he must
to scrape by alone.
Dress codes, schedules, bosses, labor,
he puts up with forced servitude
out of the purest form of love
for his woman
and for his children.

On a few special days
that mark the working man's life,
he deserves the best food and drink,
the devotion of his woman at his side,
and he deserves the companionship
of his closest allies.

Unspoken Friendship

The tattoo artist
with the dreadlocks and the comic book t-shirts,
he'd stand in front of his shop
chain smoking and drumming up business
from passersby most nights of the week.
The first few times I walked past
we ignored each other.
Eventually came the head nods,
and then the quick greetings.
The day I stopped
and asked him for a tattoo,
he chuckled and said, 'It's about time.'
Even though we had never previously spoken,
for one evening inside the tattoo shop,
that artist and I rhapsodized for hours
as old friends.

Snapped

Violence,
much like hopes and dreams,
the search for truth
and justice,
is not pursued solely by the mad.
Sometimes, the most mild-mannered person
walking down the sidewalk
can no longer absorb
the constant onslaught of attacks
doled out by life,
and suddenly,
the gun, the knife, the bomb,
they make a lot more sense.

Bus Stop Ballerina

At the bus stop,
a chubby girl of about 10 or 11
in rainbow-colored leg warmers
danced and spun around like a ballerina.
Her mother, dressed in blue hospital scrubs,
sat on the bench and watched.
A smile formed beneath her weary eyes,
revealing a small joy after a hard day.
Another woman in a business suit said,
'She does well for such a heavy girl.'
The mother politely nodded
and then pulled out her smartphone.
Her smile vanished.

Sunday Mornings

Sunday mornings
climbing out of bed
and walks to breakfast joints,
these years,
go a little slower.
Some blame the whiskey.
Others say it's age
or exhaustion from the jobs.
The rest of us,
we're too busy reflecting
on faith and our place
in the cosmos
to give a damn
about speed.

Second Class

A young man with tattoos
walked in to the bookstore café.
He cupped his chin with one hand
and examined two chairs
at the empty table
in front of me.
He silently compared the older chair
with the torn, dilapidated seat cushion
to the newer chair, that still had a black metallic shine.
He picked up the beaten chair
and carried it to the table behind me
to join his friends.

That's how we define ourselves,
our class, our place in the world.
Some people believe they deserve
the best seat in the house.
Others believe themselves second class,
commoners whose insecurities run rampant.
We do it to ourselves.

No matter which seat we take,
every one of us
knows love and hate.
We all fight and struggle.
We are all unique.
We are all the same.

Fallen Limb

A teenage boy sat alone at a picnic bench along the river,
twirling the tip of a pocket knife on the table top.
He then flipped the knife a few inches in the air
and watched as the blade landed and
stuck perfectly straight into a table plank.
A slight smile of satisfaction
pulled across his face.

When the cops came to remove the boy
from society, they found him gently carving
the bark from a fallen tree limb.
He'd planned on crafting a walking stick
for an elderly neighbor.

A week later, after the tears,
after the news coverage,
the half-carved limb remained on the ground,
next to the picnic bench,
undisturbed.

Escape

All I ever wanted
was to be left alone.
The more I ran,
the faster the cockroaches pursued
with their false friendships
and self-serving greed.

A man grows tired, sagged,
and his body slows,
his mind withers,
as death approaches.
This is not from old age,
but from thousands of stabs
delivered by forked tongues
of friends and enemies,
and his women.

As the spirit escapes
and runs
from the madness,
it's the soul which finally
has the last laugh
in the darkness,
alone.

Art is Headaches

At a sidewalk table in front of the coffee shop,
a young writer tried to explain the meaning of life.
'Life is all about recognizing the art around us.
The colors of the flowers is art,
the color of the leaves on trees,
hell, even the color of dirt is art.'

I took several long sips of coffee
while she droned on about colors.
'What about the blind?' I said.
'If art is life, and art is color,
are the blind denied life?'
'No,' she said, 'they can hear it.'

Unfortunately, so could I.

Monday Nights

Sometimes on late Monday nights
I'll climb out of bed,
get dressed,
and walk outside
into the middle of the street.
The lack of cars and people
brings peace.
It's just me,
accompanied by the steady hums
of building ventilation systems.
I often think about old friends
long gone.

Gold Coin

In front of the bar
a thin guy in an oil-stained t-shirt
pulled out a pack of cheap cigarettes
from his front jeans pocket.
'You got a light, buddy?'
I pulled out my black Zippo.
He turned his pack upside down
and a single gold coin fell into his palm
along with a half-smoked cigarette.
'What's with the coin?'
'I always carry it,' he said.
'If I drop dead,
I want the motherfucker who finds me
to have a good day.'

Summer Bridge Sidewalk

On the city bridge sidewalk
one summer night,
I contemplated
the second half of my life
among the lights
reflected upon the river.

I came to the realization
that no one will remember me.
My readers will soon forget,
as will my family.
That's why I need you,
to remember why I smile
and how I think.

Perhaps a young man with ambition
will inquire about me one day.
If that happens, pour him a drink.
Tell him I loved the sentiment
only the written word can deliver,
but I never loved words as much
as I loved you.

Birds Are Life

Walking around the city one summer Saturday
a poor artist selling bird sketches
called out to me as I approached.
'You look like a bad motherfucker.'
'Shit, I'm just a regular guy.'
I could see he wanted to sell me a sketch.
'You don't like birds, huh?'
I pulled out a ten from the wallet.
'Give me a good one.'
He handed me a beautiful hummingbird.
'Birds are life,' he said,
'and you just bought me a sandwich.'
'I didn't buy your sandwich.
The hummingbird bought it.'
'You see?' he said.
'Birds are life.'
Who was I to disagree?

Fight Greed with Truth

Dear, Robin Red Crest:
I see you've visited the tree in my front yard.
It's good to see you, my old friend.
Sometimes I wonder
what it would be like to own a bird,
but then I remember
no one really owns birds
or cats or dogs or people.

Possession is a form of control, Robin.
A growing number of living things
are falling under the control
of the gluttonous, who reach out
from the greasy troughs of office buildings.
They distract us with shiny electronics
while they wrap their fists around our lives.
We worship the greedy who choke our spirits
and despise the weak and the indigent
for not recognizing their masters.

But not you, Robin.
You are without possessions,
free to detect the suffocating grip of control.
Your wings carry you away.

The only possessions a man truly owns
are his thoughts and his heart.
My thoughts and my heart live in these words.
The whiskey in this tall glass, my form of escape,
may claim ownership of those items
before the day is over.
That's okay by me.

Self-Induced

I deluded myself into believing
the self-induced lie.
The hustlers at the bar,
the felons she and I passed on the sidewalks
when we took summer strolls at dusk,
and even the skinny hipsters in coffee shops,
they all stared at her skintight yoga pants
as they wiped the saliva
from their lonely lips.

She sauntered through the city
a blue-collar princess,
poor and modest, raised by Irish Catholics
with modest values.
That girl had the ability to lace kind words
between middle fingers and crass insults
about sluts and small peckers,
and red lipstick drags
on Marlboro lights.

She latched onto my quiet confidence
and stroked my forearm tattoos
when her pussy got wet.
I told myself I loved her body,
her eyes, her hair, her face.
The truth is, I loved her soul.
I loved her every single day
especially those nights
she fucked other men.
She was better than me,
but for a while
she kept coming
back for more.

Break Out

Standing on a street corner
on a random Wednesday
during afternoon rush hour,
one can see the despair
on the withdrawn faces
of people who attempt
to temporarily escape
their prisons
for one night.

Everyday Thrills

The sunset over the hills
behind the three rivers
really is the best way to ponder
our vast universe.
I never understood people
who are too busy bickering amongst families,
pursuing cheap celebrities,
fucking false lovers,
to ever gaze up at the stars.

People fear what we do not understand.
We ignore that which we cannot control.
I've always feared the easy answers
that minimize our lives.
Unanswered questions
are the everyday thrills
that keep us on our toes.
Exploration of new questions
to old beliefs
makes us mortal.

Self-Discovery

In the back of my Honda Element
a single mom of two
licked the tip of my cock.
The scent of her strawberry lip gloss filled the car.
Every few seconds she'd look up at me
and smile at my ridiculous facial expressions.

'You think I'm a slut,' she said
while pressing the cock against her cheek.
'Sluts are courageous.'
'What do you mean?'
'You live the life you choose.
Other cowards live as they're told.
That makes you unique, baby. Strong.'

She stared past me out the rear window
until I went mostly limp.
She then wrapped her mouth around the top half
and worked on me deep and with passion.
Sensations coursed through my body,
feelings I didn't know existed,
a level of ecstasy
I would never experience
again.

Imagine, Always

In the meadows of the countryside,
we're hypnotized by the stars
and the mysteries of the cosmos.
On sidewalks in the city,
we're hypnotized by the lights
and the mysteries of human dynamics.
No matter where we stand
when we gaze upwards
there's always space for imagination
and wonder.

Late Night Stallions

Late at night in the quiet,
when we relax the stranglehold
over our minds,
that's when our imaginations
can finally run wild
as stallions on unending beaches
within our limitless cosmos.
During these moments,
it's common to feel anxiety,
but once we leap over that wall
we are then ready
to ride free
as the heroes
of our dreams.

ACT TWO

Sidewalks

Saturday sidewalks are filled by the youthful,
the boys with young muscles and hard heads,
the girls with soft skin under short skirts.
They wander sidewalks in search of escape.
Each of them dance with lust,
drink hard,
and inject madness
into their veins.

On Sunday mornings,
after the splendor of uninhibited release,
the young weep in regret of poor choices,
their air saturated in reality.

Sidewalks then belong to the wise
who wake from a good rest.
These men and women drink roasted coffee,
reflect on a transcendent spirituality,
read great poetry,
and meet friends to discuss
the roots of democracy.

Every year, the unchanging concrete slabs
of sidewalks appear slightly different.
They reflect our perspectives.
Sidewalks that once led to freedom,
now lead to enlightenment.
In future years,
these same sidewalks
will lead to rest.

Respect

In the late 1990s, on Pittsburgh's South Side
there was a café I'd frequent
with large cozy chairs next to picture windows
that looked out onto East Carson Street,
the main drag in that part of town.

From those chairs, I'd read and write and watch
tattooed bikers, artists, skaters,
young sluts with their tits out,
and poor thugs in dirty clothes.
All of them posed as weathered statues
against brick walls.
They craved attention,
respect,
a solid footing
for their place in society.

Today, I imagine most of those people are
dead or in prisons
or barely making it
with several children
and dead-end jobs.

That café, like so many storefronts,
fell victim to the polite ravages
of suburban malls and the internet.
Those days are gone to never return.

Still, the people had my attention.
For what it's worth,
they will always have my respect.

Divine Identification

A black man in his fifties
with pockmarks all over his face
shuffled in my direction on the sidewalk.
He carried a plastic shopping bag
that appeared to contain a sweatshirt.
His pants were torn near the knee
and he wore old fashioned leather shoes
that had probably seen more miles and time
than any pair of shoes, or feet
should ever have to endure.

'Excuse me,' I said as we approached.
'I'm wondering if you're Christ.'
The man grinned, revealing yellow, decayed teeth.
'Is it that obvious?'
'Yeah, pretty much.'
'Fine. Just don't tell anyone else.'
The man then continued on his way.
I headed home
to make a sandwich.

Don't Know Me

You don't know me.
I'm warning you now,
don't even consider knowing me
or pretend to know me.
I've beaten lesser men
and poisoned the hearts
of lesser women
for trying to know me.

I am aggressively alone
in distant observation,
away from unpredictable friends
who often transform into
entirely predictable enemies.

Alone is my simple form of silent tranquility
with my thoughts and my words
and my unfulfilled dreams.

Alone is the dark silhouette
of a single Canadian goose
that stands majestically
on the shore of the summer river
below the orange city skyline at dusk.

Alone is the smell
of your old leather jacket
and a soft kiss
that partially wakes me
before you leave
in the early morning
to never return.

Lone Fisherman

A lone fisherman in his retirement years
sat in a folding chair just off the bike trail
along the Monongahela River.
'Any luck today?' I asked.
'Doesn't matter,' he said.
'I started fishing years ago
to get some time alone.
Any time I'm here I feel lucky.'
The smile across his face
proved his point.

Whiskey-Laced Sorrow

When the drunk sighs
at last call,
he is again forced to face reality,
the cold and lonely truth.
As he stumbles home
along poorly lit sidewalks,
the stench of his
whiskey-laced sorrow
is a reminder
the best years
and the best women
will never
return.

Dream the Dreams

On Sundays,
most people go to brunch with family
or take walks to lazy coffees shops
to meet with friends.
Some of us gaze out windows
to dream the dreams
we can only dream
away from the distractions
that rule our lives.

City Skyline

Gazing at the city skyline at night
through the living room window
brings peace to raging thoughts.
From a distance, all one sees are lights,
they twinkle peacefully
against a black curtain.

The rapists and the drunkards,
the hookers and the fascists,
they're all hidden in the landscape,
right below the surface.

If we allow them to seduce us,
even for one succulent moment,
they will consume every last ounce
of our reason, our purpose,
and leave us in madness.

Poignant

'You know what word I hate?'
Derek was trying to make it as a writer,
but couldn't stop talking about writing.
The way he went on about word usage
bored me to death
on the days I hung out
at the South Side café.

'What word do you hate, Derek?'
I should've known better than to ask.
Had I sat in silence,
he would've stared at me
with that crooked nose
and shallow eyes
for at least an hour...

...and I had books to read.

'Poignant,' Derek said,
'that's the most pretentious fucking word
anyone can say.'
He stared at me again.
'If something makes you sad, write sad,' he shouted
and banged his fist on the table,
almost upsetting my cup of coffee.
It was all I could do to avoid eye contact
with the douche bag.

'Your pants are pretentious,' I said.
'What?'
'You bought those jeans with holes
already torn in the legs.
You didn't earn those holes.'
Derek opened his mouth

as if to argue,
but stopped short.

'So what. You're fat,' he said.
That whining tone infuriated me
more than the cheap insult.
I dropped my copy of The Outsiders
and jumped out of the chair.
'Get the fuck up," I said,
'so I can punch your face in.'

'Calm down, big man. Sit down.'
Once I got comfortable, Derek stood.
'I'm just saying, I hate that word.'
'Poignant?'
'Don't say it!'
'Alright,' I said and chuckled.
'It hurts my ears.'
'Get the fuck away from me.'
Derek moved off.
Before he left the café
he pointed at me,
his shallow eyes narrowed, determined.
"If I see that fucking word in any book,
I'll throw it in the trash
and never read that author again.'

I hope he reads this poem
and fulfills that empty pledge.
Unfortunately, we're not usually so lucky
to lose such anti-friends
as promised.

Con Game

How does one know when he is being played?
The answer is, he doesn't know,
and chances are he'll never find out.
The best conmen get off
on selling us empty promises
of false solutions
to very real problems.

Conmen make damn sure
when the so-called remedies
only add to our existing problems,
we are so invested in the con game
that we not only defend
the empty promises
and false solutions,
we heap praise
onto the conman
for destroying our lives.

Legal Addictions

Women.
Booze.
Gambling.
These are the legal addictions
that provide us escape
out on the streets
and in the bars.
These are the addictions
of desperate men
that kill us softly
when we least
expect the
demise.

Sell Yourself

How the fuck did we get here?
That's a question I often ask myself and rarely answer.
How does a man wake up early in the morning
and then proceed to sell his body and his skills
to some job that only pays him enough to eat,
just so he won't collapse the next day?

One day in the early summer,
I walked into one of the bars.
A group of white men in khakis
celebrated some old fuck's retirement.
I watched them a while
and discovered
they didn't celebrate the man
or his lifetime of accomplishments.
Instead, they congratulated him
for his escape.

Easily Despised

The drunken bum is easily despised
for the way she appears on sidewalks,
or the way he smells in restaurants.
When we see sidewalk dwellers
dancing, lost
within the savage forest
of our pay-to-play kingdom,
many of us take comfort
in the absurd belief that we're superior.
Perhaps we scorn these souls
because we secretly know the truth,
that each of us is one financial setback
or one nervous breakdown away
from joining them.

The Show

A sexy, curvaceous red head
walked through her living room
in front of the window
of her street level apartment
on the South Side of Pittsburgh.
She wore only white and pink striped panties
and a white lace bra.

The woman walked across the room,
littered with clothing and empty glasses,
children's toys and ashtrays.
Every so often she'd stop
and turn her back to the window.
She'd run her finger inside the elastic
of the panties to show off her ass.
She performed this little routine
over and over again.

Two young men, poorly dressed degenerates,
watched her from the sidewalk,
both of them grinning ear to ear,
each of them rubbing the crotch of his sweatpants.
The occasional chuckle or catcall
escaped their quivering lips.

After a long while, a pickup truck parked
along the curb in front of the apartment building.
A man in his mid-thirties stepped out,
his clothes covered in drywall dust.
In a slow, exhausted pace,
the construction worker strolled to the window,
his eyes weary from a hard day,
a damn hard life.

After getting a good look
at the woman in the window
and the degenerates on the street,
his back straightened,
his eyes opened wide.
'What the mother fuck!' he said,
and then he bolted
for the front door of the building.

The woman quickly disappeared
from the window,
as if she never existed.
A few muffled screams,
a couple of loud thuds
rumbled out of the building.
The sounds of violence
faintly trickled onto the street.

The two young men shuffled along
the sidewalk, the show now over.
Another Thursday night
in the city.

Dominance

Along the shore of the Allegheny River in Pittsburgh
a little girl of about seven, dressed in a track suit
threw chunks of bread to nearby ducks and geese.
The geese, twice the size of their mallard brethren,
aggressively pushed between the ducks
to gobble up each morsel.

The girl placed her hands on her hips
and scolded the winged despots for their greed.
A few of the ducks joined in the protest,
and quacked in solidarity, for justice.
The geese remained undeterred
in their conquest.

Clearly frustrated, the little girl gave up.
She handed the bag of bread to her mother
and then ran off to join a group of older children
playing frisbee in a nearby grass field.
The ruling geese and the victimized ducks
continued to swim near the shore,
hungry and confused,
and without that reliable food source.

Mall Rat Fascism

Outside one of Pittsburgh's many suburban malls
on a warm spring Saturday,
three teenage boys leaned against the wall
near the entrance of a department store.
One teenager wore a red t-shirt
with a distressed print of the confederate flag.
Around each of them hung a dark aura,
a vibe of undisturbed violence
that yearned to break free.

On the same sidewalk, a middle-aged woman
wearing a colorful hijab and a long dress
held the hand of a little boy of about eight.
They strolled toward the entrance of the store.
The little boy jumped and giggled,
but the woman held a stern expression
that conveyed both concern
and annoyance.

The teenagers stood up straight,
they took their hands out of their pockets,
and watched the woman with intensity.
"Get back to Syria," one shouted.
The others laughed
in roars of contempt,
a mocking kind of rage
that exerted dominance
over the sidewalk.

The little boy's mood turned to sorrow.
He hugged that woman's leg
and buried his face in the silky material
of her dress.
He sobbed loudly, humiliated,

his cries filled with fear
his tears laced with shame.
For what was probably the first time
in his short life,
he felt despised.

"Shhh," the woman said in a calming tone
and rubbed his back
while the teenagers continued to laugh
and scream in a kind of hysterical seizure.
Phrases like "sand nigger,"
"terrorist," and "whore"
echoed through the parking lot.

Without acknowledging the young men,
the woman coaxed the little boy out of her dress,
she pulled him close to her side,
and quickly walked him back the way they came.
The little boy's sobs then hushed to a whimper
and he wiped away the tears
with his free hand.

Once the woman and boy turned the corner,
the dark aura of hatred around the teenagers
crept back under the surface from where it came.
The one wrapped in the Confederate flag
formed a wide sneer across his face,
an expression that reflected the raw euphoria of power.
He then casually placed his hands behind his head
and leaned back against the wall
in victory.

What is the Point?

What is the point?
We go to some God forsaken job,
We listen to the demands of some boss.
We kill ourselves, slowly
for a few bucks and validation,
both of which buys us little,
both of which really doesn't belong to us.
At least we have each other,
or at least we did,
until the bosses learned how
to rip us apart with politics.
Now we suffer alone,
and all around us
are enemies.

Dystopic Truth

Walking in the used bookstore
on the hunt for a rare Bukowski collection,
I held the door open
for a young woman walking out.
Propagandized with the ever-present threat
of rape and sexual harassment,
she refused to make eye contact
or recognize the kind act.
Instead, she looked at the ground
in totalitarian fear
and walked past.
I didn't feel slighted,
just ashamed
for myself,
for our culture.
The sad truth of modern life
is that we live and breathe
dystopia.

Sidewalk Cat

Out for a walk one Saturday morning
I passed an antique store.
In the window sat a cat
with an all white fluffy coat.
The cat appeared hardened,
probably from a life of confinement,
and from the daily onslaught of customers
that insist on petting its furry back.

I stopped at the window
and that cat gave me a good once over.
He and I were compatriots in a mad world,
both of us shamed for our truths,
both of us loved in convenient moments.
After a minute, I moved on
to grab a coffee and a cigar,
secure in the knowledge
I'd made a new friend.

Live Forever

In our young adult years,
the novelty of liberation
sparked our imaginations.
We stayed out all night
in diners and on the streets.
We fucked whomever we chose
without fear
of manmade consequences.
We penned horrible stories,
painted absurd portraits,
and drew the weakest comics.
Still, we were free spirits
with fresh souls
that we truly believed
would live forever.

Lonely Diners

A man sits diagonally in front of me
to my left in the diner.
Over his shoulder, I see
he's navigating Facebook
on a cheap laptop.
Behind him, I'm writing this poem.
Every 13 seconds a notification rings.
He has a Facebook message.
The notifications are messages from a woman.
She types heart shapes in place of words.
It is the standard online flirtation
that has replaced real relationships.
He is quite popular
as he eats toast with purple jelly
and sits alone.

People once came to diners
to chain smoke cigarettes
and drink pots of coffee
and think
and talk
and read poetry.
We didn't have much,
but we had each other.
Now we're individuals
who sit in silence
alone.

Some of us get chat notifications.
Some of us write poems.
All of us still get the coffee
and the toast
with purple jelly.

Suicide Addiction

On barstools, people drone on endlessly
about meditation and yoga and hot yoga
or cold jogging, and bicycling in special pants.
'It gives you a high,' they say.
'You're on top of the world,' they scream.
The saps push their new religions
with the gusto of car salesmen.
When it's a woman, I politely listen
between mouthfuls of whiskey and ginger ale.
When it's a man, I shut him down
early in his ramble. I tell him to
grow a pair.

Curvaceous women with long hair
and cunts that easily get wet,
bourbon that melts the top layer of ice,
pocketing a few bucks after sinking the 8 ball,
those are the suicide addictions,
I tell punks,
that give a man small escapes,
the sins he needs to commit
in order to feel whole.
A man who knows the desperation
of fulfilling temptations always
works harder to stay one step ahead
of the game.

Weaponized

I don't understand.
You claim to be a moral person,
but I saw you ignore that bum on the corner.
I heard you say 'the blacks' are the problem.
I watched you feel your own crotch
when the 12 year old girl walked by
in that restaurant.

Some say you're a good guy,
because they see you quietly
commute to the job and watch sports.
Others say they can reason with you,
and your 'misinformed' view of the world
over drinks at happy hour.

You and I, we know different,
because we're both acquainted with the underbelly
of society, and our fellow degenerates know
your thoughts are poisoned
by the media, the internet, politicians.
Your mind has become weaponized,
your body is a ticking time bomb,
and it's going to detonate
at any moment.

When it Rains

When it rains,
whiskey induced thoughts
wander in lust.
The most powerful memories
of love and hate,
losses and gains,
rise to the surface.
That steady patter
contrasts
the chaos
we live.

Denial

My thoughts
never dwell on you.
Memories of shared laughs
over the pool table
and the arguments
from the old days in school,
they've all been erased.
I never reflect on your life
or our friendship,
not even when I see
random tree branches
reach for the sun
much like your arms that day
when the doctor lied
about how that terrible disease
was gone.

Bogie

An old man dressed in a suit
and holding a wooden cane
leaned back against the brick wall
of the local bank
as I crossed the street
to hit the ATM machine.

Once I stepped up on the curb,
he nodded to me in a cool cat manner,
like Humphrey Bogart,
who didn't sweat the petty schedules
and the absurd pursuits
that consume the rest of us.

His smile pushed
away the crease lines
of his weathered face
to reveal a simple joy
I will always remember
and hope to repeat
later in life.

Neglected

I only love you
at night,
when loneliness
fuels desire
and
desperation
replaces
rational thought.

Your value is reflected
in an empty whiskey bottle,
sideways
on the stained carpet.

Funny how everything
is eventually
neglected.

Short Life

The moment I begin to care
about the opinions
and groupthink of other people,
that's the moment I've failed
at this short life.
Scream from atop the mountain.
Fuck and love, work and sacrifice,
and never forget the experiences
that make your truth.
In the end, all that matters
are the best memories of
the tastiest pussy,
the hard fought battles,
and so many wonderfully
drunken adventures.

See Inside

On sidewalks,
some people smile
as I walk past.
Most others pretend
to not see me,
but I see them.
I see their sadness,
their insecurities.

Surrogate Grandmother

In front of me in the café
an older woman, about 70 or 75 years old
sat facing me at a table across the room.
She sat alone and read the newspaper
with a flat, contented look on her face.
I stopped clacking at a story on the typer
to study the woman.

A walker with wheels was parked next to her.
On the front of the walker hung a bag,
maybe you'd call it a large purse,
with embroidered print on the front
that read, 'Here Comes Treble'
next to an embroidered musical note.
The old woman wore a loud blue print t-shirt
with text that read,
'You are about to exceed
the limits of my medication.'

I immediately and silently
adopted this woman
as my grandmother.
I couldn't imagine
a more perfectly chaotic
woman to share a pot of soup
while listening intently
to her stories.

Confidence

When I glance at store windows
while strolling on sidewalks
the reflection of an accomplished man
stares back.

The man in the window,
he's fat, bald, gray in the beard,
but there's a spark of magic
in his blue-green eyes,
a sense of wisdom passed on
from his fathers before him.

The man in the window,
he's a badass lover, a sinner,
a fighter, a loyal friend.
He remembers the time
you clasped his hand
as he battled
the lynch mob's popular rage
for daring to voice an opposing view.
He will never forget
your courage.

Fortitude

There's something peculiar
about witnessing courage
in the face of hatred.
True righteousness hits me deep.
It flourishes from within,
the way epiphanies bloom in scholars
or the way love overwhelms
young students.

There's majesty in the underdog
who stands until his knees buckle,
who shouts until her voice breaks,
fueled only by fortitude,
mocked for feeling empathy,
hated for living truth.

In moments of moral principle
I see peace amidst the chaos
poetry amidst the prose
in the eyes of the young
and in the old
who fight
for justice.

Minerals and Violence

Sitting in traditional wooden pews
back in the mid-2000s,
a guest priest from the heart of the Congo
delivered a homily in broken English
about how his country had been torn to shreds
by warlords who control that region's
vast and valuable mineral deposits.

As the priest spoke in gentle passion,
a sea of sympathetic white faces listened
to him describe the rapes and murders,
the poverty and oppression.
One middle-aged woman in a yellow dress near the front
quietly sobbed at the reminder of true suffering,
a torture greater than mere death.

Out of a sense of courtesy
or possible humble generosity,
the priest did not disclose the minerals
that had brought on such gluttonous violence
were the very elements that make our electronics
flash and glow as perpetual escapes.

Instead, the priest requested
we pray with him
for future mystical solutions
to immediate physical problems.

As we filed out of the church
the older woman who'd wept
discussed driving to the local mall.
Apparently, there'd been a sale on mobile phones.
The crisp spring breeze had dried our tears,
and the power of the almighty dollar

wiped away our curiosity
and our short-term memories.

ACT THREE

ACT THREE

Today

Today depression visited
a quiet hopelessness one feels
from yet another grave injustice
that cannot be rectified
without mass support
within empire.

Driving home from the job,
the world fell silent.
On one street corner
stood a man of color
in dirty work pants
He frowned behind a gray beard,
his eyes distant.

He and I, we shared a truth
that while the poor
continue to weep
for what will be their early deaths,
those who represent hatred
celebrated
again.

Leather Bag

This leather bag and I,
we've tasted a bit of the world
on dirt trails and city sidewalks,
inside cars, buses, and planes.
This leather bag and I have done battle together.
We've struck intellectual blows in classrooms,
and we've celebrated success in board rooms.
The bag and I even laugh about that time
it blocked a drunk's fist aimed at my kidneys.

Few people believe in the loyalty of a bag.
They seek devotion from others,
toxic love from all the wrong places,
only to suffer the greatest disappointments.

This leather bag and I,
we're the best of friends.
That's how it is
and that's how it will always be.

Old Wisdom

In a building recess
between a whiskey bar and a vape shop
an old man sat on a rolled blanket.
He held a simple sign on a torn sheet of cardboard
that read "HUNGRY."
The old man's face contained hundreds of deep crevices,
a lifetime of memories permanently imprinted,
much like the etchings found on old vinyl records.

A young man in a while golf shirt
stumbled out of the whiskey bar.
He stopped in front of the old bum to regain his balance.
'Get a job,' he said in slurred contempt.
'Do something with your life.'

The old man stared through the drunkard,
and in total silence,
that old man's worn face filled the sidewalk
with the music of his wisdom,
his pain, his experiences.
The drunkard stumbled along,
deaf to that solemn gift
of truth.

Vertical Moods

Sitting in the bar on a slow night,
a young robotics engineer from Europe
attending graduate school in Pittsburgh,
lamented about American politics.
'I don't know what's going to happen,'
he said. 'There's nothing we can do.'
'Wait a minute,' I said.
'Aren't you developing vertical farming technology?'
'Yes, that's right.'
'So the poor can feed themselves?'
'Definitely.'
'Sounds to me that you're doing plenty.'
The young friend didn't reply,
and instead took a pull from his beer.
A minute later he laughed hard
at something on the television.
He wore a permanent smile
for the rest of the night.

Bad Motherfuckers

If you let the bastards get you down,
you deserve to be down.
It's that simple.
While the mad howl
into the void
of restless summer nights,
bad motherfuckers
sip cool drinks
in confident silence.

Bad motherfuckers
laugh when others weep,
feast when others hunger,
they fuck long and deep
the angels others crave.

Bad motherfuckers die
far more often,
worn from the continual fight,
broken by the drama
of never-ending
women.

In rebirth,
bad motherfuckers learn
to wring out every last drop
of a whiskey flawed life.
Then and only then
do blood red skies,
that musky scent of wet cunt,
or these typed words
have any real meaning
or significance.

Replaced

Walking home from dinner
I learned a robot was granted citizenship
in Saudi Arabia.
That's the moment I realized
humanity had reached its pinnacle
of freedom and passion
during the struggle for civil rights,
the sexual revolution, and the women's movement
that all went down in the 1960s.

Fifty years later, the greed of robotic automation
has robbed workers of their dignity,
replaced with toxic authoritarianism,
the futile attempt to control our destinies.
Gripped by overwhelming fear of our own demise,
we dress up our thirst for totalitarianism
as feminism or masculinity.

Fifty years from now,
as robots learn to emulate emotion and intuition,
they will replace our sexual partners,
our spouses, our friends.
Our generation will sit quietly in nursing homes,
and we will wonder
what the fuck happened
that humanity allowed itself
to be so easily replaced.

Crinkled

A young man with dirty hands
and tired eyes
walked into the bar.
He sat next to a blonde
of about the same age
and ordered a beer.
'Don't even try to talk to me,'
she said loud enough for everyone to hear.
The young man didn't speak.
Defeated, he climbed off the stool.
He took a pull from the beer
and then dropped a crinkled fiver.
As he walked out the door,
the girl laughed out loud.
She showed us all
who was boss.

Wildflowers Poisoned

The deep sadness of enemies
lurks all around us,
among neighborhood streets.
It is a foul stench of rotting fish
on the shores of great lakes
that overflow with diseased tears.
It is the feeling of loss deep within the darkest forest
under an endless canopy of hateful eyes.

Souls that once embodied the beauty,
the acceptance of a vast field of wildflowers
are now poisoned, convinced
those once loved have become villains.

The wildflowers' brilliant petals,
now replaced with the most toxic thorns,
serve the interests of forces
who thirst for power
at the expense of the very fields
they've polluted.

Voyeurism

Everybody in their cars
and on the sidewalks
gawks at the train wreck,
the car crash, the big fire.
Most have no idea why.
It's simple, really.
We must constantly feel
life
or lose it.

Color Inside the Lines

I dare not allow myself to think
on Tuesday nights, alone.
It's far better to cook a meal,
listen to music, talk to the neighbors,
watch mindless political debates,
and work out in gyms.

As long as the mind is occupied
we will not contemplate our prisons.
Revolt, a distant memory, never comes.

So, sleep long and deep, my baby.
Do not awaken to the truth.
Accept what is canon,
conform to the conventional.
The fools who rub their eyes for clarity
to gaze at a possible new dawn,
always have their big, pretty eyes
ripped from their sockets
by the brave patriots
of tradition.

How dare we dream and imagine
and live free.

Red Dream

A young woman stands on the sidewalk
in front of a vape shop.
Her long red hair is the dream
of desperate men
that flutters in the cool spring breeze.
She fiddles with her smartphone,
her thumb quickly scrolls screens
in an attempt to fight boredom.
She's waiting, waiting, waiting
for her next adventure,
but those skin tight yoga pants
and her filthy sneakers tell me
she has a long wait.

Apology

I opened the door at a diner
to step out onto the sidewalk
after a late night meal.
A cold blast of winter air
startled a guy who stood five feet away.
"Sorry," he said, without really looking at me,
as if the word was a knee-jerk response
that lacked any thought or meaning.

Days later, I still had no idea
why the guy apologized.
In the social media age,
kindness and humility
have been replaced
with intimidation, approval,
and the seductive allure
of narcissistic validation.

Imperfections

I don't just love you;
I love your imperfections,
those hard memories
beneath kind eyes,
when I watch you
gaze out my window
onto the streets
and busy sidewalks
of the city
every morning.

Firsthand

One autumn day on a stroll to the cigar shop
I sought out dead leaves on the sidewalk
and stepped on them
for that satisfying potato chip crunch.
A little boy, who stood with his parents
near the entrance of a restaurant,
stared at my peculiar walking style,
with squinted eyes and a crinkled nose
as if I were crazy.

After picking up a 60 gauge acid,
I stood on the corner to light up.
That's when I saw the same family
walking in my direction,
and that damn kid purposely stepped
on every dried leaf he could find
for that satisfying potato chip crunch.

I blew a large cloud of smoke
as they approached,
so that kid would know he was being watched.
My only hope is that he learned
there's often a world of difference
between what we observe
and what we experience
firsthand.

Cupcake Victory

In the bookstore cafe,
an old man in a dirty blue winter coat
struggled to eat an oversized chocolate cupcake
and sip at a small coffee.
His hands and thighs shook uncontrollably
as he focused more on safeguarding
his dignity, by not smearing the frosting
across his wrinkled face,
rather than enjoying the expensive treat.
The mall rats at neighboring tables
wore expressions of pity
for the man,
for his limitations.
He and I, we knew the truth,
that once he finished that cupcake
and downed that coffee,
he moved on with his day
a champion.

Bourbon Break

The moment the mind floats
on two shots of bourbon
our physical and mental ailments,
the stress of bills, the job,
and our resentment for ex-lovers
clocks out for the evening.
Don't worry.
The shit storm will return
in the morning,
but that break,
a stroll around the neighborhood,
and a quick prayer
gives us the tools
to withstand the storm.

Departed

Coffee on Monday mornings,
reclaiming a familiar routine
after a depressing week,
carries a richer aroma
and a sweeter flavor
than the same brew
in the same cup
any other time of our lives.

If our minds, our experiences
define so many of our tastes,
consider the satisfying joy a handshake
brings to a lonely old hermit.

Imagine the luscious splendor
of a long walk during a summer drizzle
after the endless confinements
of hospitals and doctors,
and finally the funeral home
when she departed this realm.

Near Miss

In city traffic one fall morning,
a driver of a rusted white sedan,
probably on the way to a job,
sped through a red light
near a school zone.

A woman in pink sweat pants
grabbed the backpack attached to her young son
and yanked him close
as the sedan swerved in the crosswalk
at the last moment
before obliterating them both
on the street.

In bars and in churches
and all over social media,
we question our violent culture.
No one seems to have the answers,
yet we ignore the simple truth.
We're expected to suspend our humanity,
to kill anyone who crosses our paths
for the privilege to work and earn,
all so we can eat.

Preach

Sometimes a writer will make contact
and ask me for advice.
No matter the phrasing of the question,
the response is always the same.

Live your TRUTH.

One must stand up to the wave of greed
in today's world of keyboard warriors online
that spew hate behind smartphones.
Poisonous lovers are more easily tempted
to seek greener fields.
Bosses, stressed out by bad economics
adopt entitled attitudes to control.

None of these entities,
not a single one of these people
have the privilege
to cage you.
You are an animal.
You are powerful!

Know your motherfucking truth,
whatever that may be,
and live free.

All I Can Do

I sit here at the table
in the dark,
the glow from the cityscape
outside the window gently reflects
off my glass of cheap bourbon
and ginger ale.

In the bedroom,
my loving girlfriend is fast asleep.
We both have work in the morning,
in a few hours,
but I can't sleep.

With every sip of whiskey, my right eye twitches.
Today, a brother I'll never meet was gunned down.
Yesterday, a sister was ran over by a Dodge sedan.
Tonight, I drink and think and pray,
because that's all I can do.
That's all any of us can do.

Groundhog Utopia

Sweating and hungry
on a humid summer afternoon,
hundreds of day job workers
sat in a line of traffic,
waiting impatiently
for the light to turn green.
Along the side of the road,
a groundhog sat upright in the tall grass
and he feasted on a patch of weeds.

The groundhog didn't have a mortgage to pay.
He didn't have to navigate through a world
of bosses and bills,
politics and war.
He appeared to live
a quiet, content life,
concerned only about simple
groundhog troubles.

When the groundhog finished eating,
he stared at a guy behind the wheel
of a plain gray sedan,
his eyes carried a sense of pity
for the human imprisoned in a cage on wheels.
After a moment of examining the people,
the groundhog appeared to grow bored,
and so he scurried into the tall grass,
probably for a good shit and a nap.

Three Weeks In

About three weeks in
to one of the many jobs
the boss stormed up to me
like she meant business.
'You don't act professional!'
she screamed in an emotional rant.
'You don't dress professional
and your humor isn't professional!'

I stared at her in silence,
occasionally feeling my eyelids blink.
When she finished, I asked a simple question:
'Can you define professional?'

She stormed away
with the ferocity
in which she arrived.

I was back on the job boards
that night.

Kicked Around

In October 2016,
during a heated presidential campaign,
I took a day off work
and walked over to a local coffee shop.
It was particularly sunny for the time of year,
so I decided to sit at a sidewalk table
and watch the world go by.

After ten minutes or so of watching the cars,
retired dog walkers, and young couples,
a thirty-something guy approached.
'You got a lighter, buddy,' he said
holding an unlit cigarette.
Thin, lanky, the guy was dressed
in a stained corporate giveaway t-shirt
that advertised a walkathon from 2006.
'Nope,' I said. 'Sorry, brother.'

He flopped into the chair on the other side of my table.
'Fuck this shit," he said.
'How's a guy supposed to smoke
when no one else smokes?'
I didn't have a response.

'The world ain't my world anymore, you know?'
'It's a world for the tech geeks,' I said.
He scanned the sidewalk around us.
'You sure you don't have a light?'
'I wouldn't lie to you.'

'So who you voting for?' I asked.
If two strangers were going to sit together,
we'd might as well get real.
'I don't know, probably Trump.'

He drummed the table
with what I took as nervous energy.
'Why did you ask me that?'
'Just curious.'
'Well, I'm sick of getting kicked around.'
'Yeah?'
'I don't even have money for a lighter.
Obama didn't do anything good.
I fucking hate Clinton.'

'How about Bernie Sanders?' I said.
'Eh. I don't know. He's okay for an old commie.
I think we just need to blow it all up.
Drop a nuke on the world and start over.'
'Fuck, brother, that's pretty harsh,' I said.
'I ain't your brother.'

The guy stood up and stepped onto the sidewalk.
'I'll get a light somewhere else.'
He then jogged across the street
and disappeared into the crowd.

I pulled out my smartphone
and typed out a text message to the girlfriend.
'I think the political and corporate establishment
finally found a way to take us down.
We better get ready.'

After a couple minutes.
the phone vibrated on top of the table.
She replied with one word.
'Duh.'

Temporary Solutions

A lot of shit goes down on sidewalks.
The most desperate souls
sell their bodies and their spirits
for a little bread that only leads
to temporary solutions, escapes
from everlasting problems.
They seek what they will never find,
peace within the landscape,
among the masses who profit
from their predictable failures
and untimely deaths.

Black Friday

For many years on the Friday after Thanksgiving
my oldest friend and I,
along with about one hundred other heavy readers,
stood on the sidewalk before dawn's first light
in front of a local used bookstore.
While we patiently waited in the freezing cold
for the shop to open, the manager gave us hot coffee
and his appreciation for our mutual passion
of the written word.

Huddled in shivering groups,
we allies of imagination discussed poetry,
comics, novels, and the world's rich history.
While serious shoppers trampled each other
over big screen televisions and trendy new toys
inside mall electronics stores,
we found comfort, friendship
in our celebration of literature.

Parole

"Running out the clock"
is maybe the most common term
in American working life.
Trapped, financially imprisoned
between four walls of servitude
on a late Friday afternoon,
we wait impatiently
for our parole from the crimes
our owners regularly commit.

Middle-Aged Vomit

Watching young hipsters
in the coffee shop
pretending to know the world,
our history, the truth of humanity,
makes a middle-aged writer
want to vomit in a paper coffee cup.
Maybe it's the way they awkwardly readjust
the mall clothes
reasonable people
could never afford to buy.
Maybe it's the mindless arrogance
reasonable people
could never afford to adopt.
Either way, the vomit is choked back,
if for no other reason than because
some minimum wage working bloke
will have to mop it up.

Consumer Survey

At the mall two weeks
before Christmas,
an army of American consumers
window shop, they browse,
they survey the battlefield.
Young women with similar shoes,
and similar hair, and similar politics
huddle in groups to plan
the impending attack.
Their body language indicates confidence.
The best goods will be captured at any cost.
Victory will be theirs.

Three Days

I once loved a woman
unconditionally
for three days.
In that short time
we ate great food and took long walks.
We fucked like champions.

When our affair fizzled,
she said I used her for sex.
I actually used her to give me a reason
to exist, beyond the grind of the job,
or these scribbled poems.

For three wonderful days,
that woman
gave me life.

Media Withdrawal

One winter day I didn't have web access.
The typer was in the shop having a virus removed,
and then I dropped the phone on pavement.
The withdrawal symptoms of lost media
were all too real.
I tried reading some Ginsberg.
That helped me forget
about Facebook and Instagram,
but after 20 minutes the fire ants came.
They crawled behind my eyes
until the words on the page no longer held any meaning.
I went for a walk in the snow
to occupy my mind and body.
An old man walked by,
he pulled a cart of groceries.
'Excuse me,' I said. 'Do you have a smartphone?'
He laughed. 'I can't afford those things.'
'Yeah, I don't think I can either.'

Serpents

Upon the soot-barren landscape
where serpents slither
in misery,
there are champions
of struggle
among the few trees
that defiantly grow
through the most toxic pollution.
We must only close our eyes
and open our minds
to sense them.

Hunted

We are the hunted,
the hated
who run in packs,
separate but equal,
rarely together,
but with similar purpose,
a singular goal,
to make it
through life.

We are despised
for our existence.
Some are fat, yet starved.
Others are slutty and ravenous.
Every day is a struggle.
We fuck and feast,
fight and pray,
and too often
we lose.

Love is fleeting,
never predictable.
It's the knowledge, you see.
We are but temporary
lovers, workers, friends.
That truth brings about
the sadness,
the madness,
the end.

Those of us who thirst
for unique perspectives
quietly celebrate life's little endings
while others mourn the loss.
Conclusions mark the end
of an experience.
We take a breath,
and then move forward
to rediscover our worlds,
forever changed.

About the Author

Ron Gavalik is a writer
in Pittsburgh, Pennsylvania.
You can stalk him online.
He likes whiskey.

Made in the USA
Middletown, DE
24 April 2022

64711875R00076